OANA HANGANU

VALENTINA DICU

CULTURAL AWARENESS GUIDE FOR EXPATS WORKING IN ROMANIA

Cover design:
Adriana Hanganu adipixdesign.com

ISBN-13: 978-1981917877
ISBN-10: 198191787X

Bucharest, 2017

TABLE OF CONTENTS

Why this book?

We decided to write this book because over the years we have observed that foreigners, especially those living and working in our country, have misunderstood Romanians.

In order to really understand someone from a different culture, one has to first appreciate the different political context and background, that is the cultural value profile of that nation. Hence, to understand the Romanian people and their behavior in both social contexts and business settings as well as identify the particularities of their work and management styles, we have to look closely at the Romanian people's background, values and historical and political contexts.

Our intention for this book is to be used as a guide and also as a workbook. The first part is a discussion on the historical background of our nation, while the second part is intended to be a practical guide for foreigners that move to Romania to lead or work in local teams. We provide a lot of insight into local people for you to form a personal opinion and draw your own conclusions.

We hope that our book will be especially helpful to newcomers to Romania as well as those who have lived here for a while and wish to improve further their understanding of local people and become more culturally aware. Our explanations should be able to clarify to expats why Romanian people act in certain ways in specific situations.

Why is it important to become culturally aware?

Cultural awareness is the foundation of good communication. It means we can step back and become aware of our cultural values, beliefs and perceptions.

This becomes central when we have to interact with people from other cultures. Being culturally aware means understanding your own cultural values, preferences and assumptions about your country of origin in order to know how local people think and why. It also means being open to learn about other cultures where one has to live and work.

We have to be open to understanding others because differences are often key factors to success. People see, interpret and evaluate things in different ways. Some behavioral patterns that in one culture may be viewed as problematic can be the norm in other cultures.

Each type of culture (monochronic or polychronic) has its own characteristics and an awareness of these differences and the blending between the two types can help or hinder communication significantly when working in an international environment.

Each national culture influences the corporate world, often having an invisible impact on the success or failure of a multinational endeavor. These invisible traits can contribute to its growth or decisively derail its plans. Being aware of the strengths and weaknesses of the most important resource of a company, its personnel, is crucial for a company to survive in an international business environment.

What Is The Culture Of A Country?

According to UNESCO, "Culture is that complex whole which includes knowledge, beliefs, arts, morals, laws, customs, and any other capabilities and habits acquired by [a human] as a member of society."

Culture brings together "a series of distinct characteristics of a particular society or social group in what means spiritual, material, intellectual or emotional terms."

It represents the knowledge of a certain group of people linked to its spoken language, its religion, its culinary/social habits, its music and arts. Culture also represents a heritage that is forwarded through specific verbal or non-verbal communication codes, in writing, by family, through art and in the mass media (press, radio, TV).

The Centre for Advanced Research on Language

Acquisition defines culture as being a sum of the common patterns of behaviors and interactions, of cognitive constructions and of understanding, which are finally acquired through the socialization process, according to livescience.com.

Therefore, culture stands for the identity of an extended social group and is favored by its unique social patterns. It is also present within the collective subconscious of one group of people and gathers the value system upon which those people are guided.

In every culture, there is a system of principles of what is desirable, and this determines the psychological profile of its members.

According to Hall (1976), the culture pattern of a country has two parts. The external culture (10%) encompasses its arts, music, literature, language, food, habits, festivals, dance, dress code and facial expressions, while the internal culture (90%) encompasses a lot more, such as its rules and norms, attitudes, beliefs, perceptions, assumptions, desires, values, expectations, views on raising children, approach to problem solving, emotional responses, concept of fairness, concept of justice and so on.

We call this the Cultural Iceberg. The external culture is part of the conscious mind and the internal culture is part of the subconscious mind.

THE CULTURAL ICEBERG

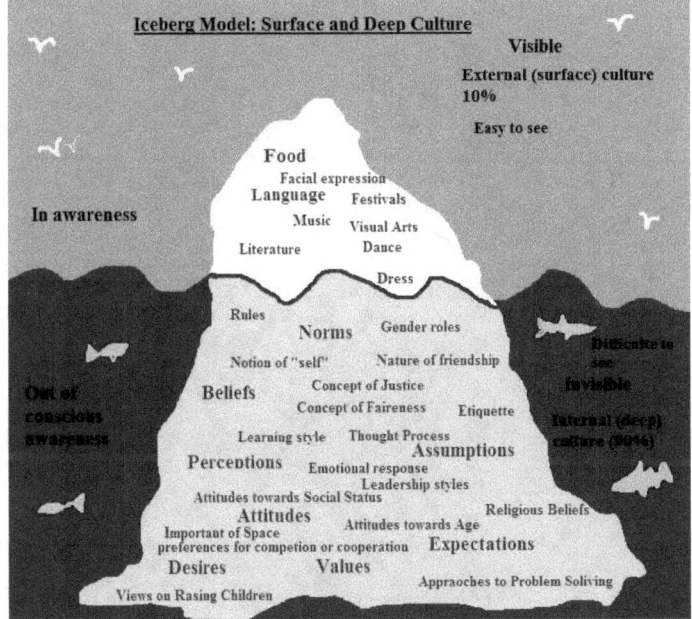

Source: culturalconflict.wordpress.com

This picture is helpful when thinking of becoming aware of another culture. The unseen part of it is harder to detect, and not being aware of this could prevent us from understanding others or being understood, thereby hampering our communication flow in a different environment.

Working Across Cultures

Moving to a new country places a great deal of stress on a person, who has to adjust to this change in environment. All those unknown administrative issues that one has to handle when moving to a new country add to this stress, but these are of a limited timeframe.

Other more important aspects of moving to another country present greater challenges such as the way in which the family integrates into the local culture. These aspects must be addressed on a daily basis, making it important to learn as much as you can about what to expect when moving to a new location, even before arriving there.

For instance, adapting to a new school environment and making new friends place a great deal of stress on children leaving old friends behind. This is a hard thing for young children to deal with while immersed in a delicate development period. Similarly, for parents integrating into the local work culture and finding new friends with whom to share their experiences are sensitive issues that affect the success or failure of the new assignment and the happiness of the family in the new location in the long run.

Taking into account all the aspects described above, our guidelines show what to consider when moving to a new country. It is important to know what to expect if you are new to the expat community as well as to realize how many aspects besides the new job are involved in such a move.

This is especially crucial when one has to integrate into a new team or manage a team of another nationality or a multiple nationality team.

To succeed in such a situation, one needs to be able to go beyond culture to understand the new environment. Newcomers have to be aware of the new country's cultural dimensions and understand its cultural differences as well as plan how to handle new challenges to achieve success.

To show what we mean, we use the Richard Lewis model of understanding a country's cultural type (termed the RLM hereafter). Richard Lewis – the author of the book "When teams collide" – developed an intuitive way of approaching this challenge to obtain success.

His approach takes into account team members, the team leader, the context and the reality of cross-cultural business conduct.

The RLM considers the following:

-      Communication and interaction patterns
-      Leadership styles
-      Meeting patterns
-      Empathy
-      Trust
-      Business ethics

All these aspects make it easier for us to understand and adapt to intercultural relations. When the members of a multicultural team work together and care for each other's personal success, then the team is well integrated and pursue a common goal.

Managers and leaders of such teams have to not only be competent in doing their jobs, but also be adaptable, open to understand local culture, have the willingness to learn, have flexibility, fairness, ability to motivate and support their teams as well as each individual member.

They have to be the "bridge" between the company policy and its established targets and local reality and have to find ways to achieve the company goals in any environment, working across cultures and achieving their personal goals at the same time.

Understanding The Cultural Type – The Richard Lewis Model (RLM)

Cultural categories of communication according to Lewis source Lewis (2005, p.89)

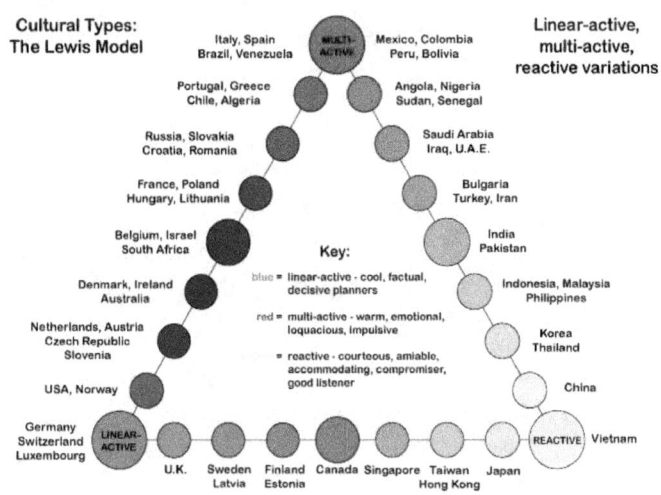

Categorizing cultures and communication styles according to RLM

In linear active cultures, people:

- Are task-oriented
- Are highly organized planners
- Do one thing at a time (linear agenda)
- Use speech for information based on facts and figures

In multi-active cultures, people:

- Are emotional and impulsive
- Attach great importance to family, meetings and relationships
- Show compassion and warmth to other
- Do many things at the same time
- Are poor followers of agendas
- Use speech for opinions

In reactive cultures, people:

- Are good listeners
- Show action or discussion
- Prefer first to listen, let the other person establish his/her position; then, disclose their opinion
- Listen before they do anything
- Use speech for harmony

This model can also be applied to individual people. People from a certain culture often do not fit entirely to the cultural profile of their own country. For example, usually women are more multi-active than men are.

The place where the member is situated on the RLM diagram is called "Cultural Anchorage" and this signifies where each person feels comfortable.

This is similar to the complementary concept of the "comfort zone", a place where we feel comfortable and reluctant to leave. The personal comfort zone has to be individually established and challenged for each individual to grow. The "magic" happens outside our comfort zones.

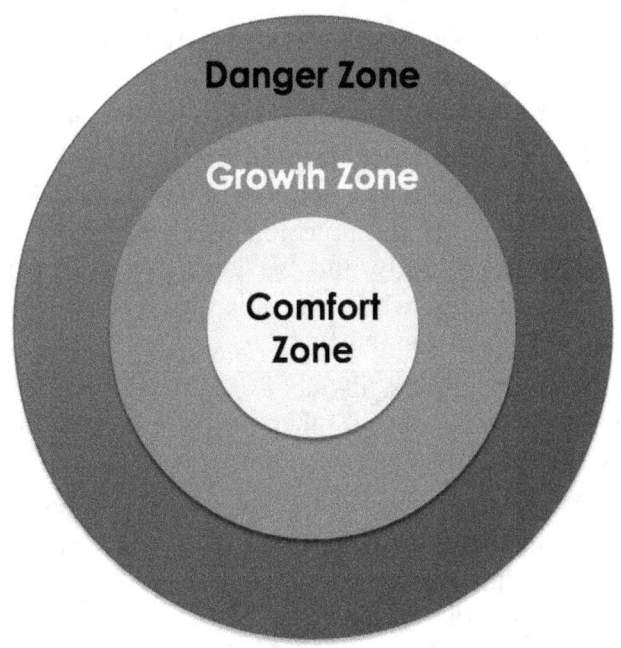

The Comfort Zone

When working in a multicultural team, the challenge is to determine each member's personal "cultural anchorage" and "comfort zone" and help them go beyond these limitations. It takes a team effort to be able to identify these critical behavioral factors, and at the same time we need to become aware of our own biases and limitations.

Most people are unaware of some aspects of their own culture when compared to others, but they can always quickly spot local cultural aspects different from their own . For an outsider, it is easier to identify the differentiating characteristics of a new culture.

However, to understand why and how local people do what they do, we need a long time to interact with the local culture to absorb knowledge of locals' past.

The easiest way to achieve all in a short time is to carry out a cultural awareness training, which allows a newcomer to concentrate on his/her job and to integrate more easily into the local culture and start doing their job while assimilating the knowledge offered by such training.

Such training offers tips about the local environment that a newcomer would otherwise take a long time to observe.

For example, for the outsiders, some cultures seem cold, organized and disciplined (Germany), while others seem too emotional (Italians) or chaotic and volatile (Nigerian).

For this reason, the role of a manager / leader is to bring all these differences together and lead the team to success.

To do that by embracing diversity rather than eliminating differences as well as finding the strong and weak points of each member and using them accordingly, it is important to know the national values of the local team or of each member of a culturally diverse team.

The manager has to be able to offer team members different perspectives than just those encouraged by the local culture.

To motivate their teams, managers and leaders have to be a live example of what they "preach." New managers must communicate clearly to make themselves understood to new teams. That is why it is important to be aware of the local language and communication style – it always helps to take lessons in the local language.

Although English is mostly used for international communication and in business, one must learn how to project the local style when communicating with local teams.

Humor is one "weapon" that goes across cultures; however, the kinds of jokes that are appropriate to make are also influenced by the cultural characteristics.

Romanian History And Geopolitical Context

Geography and important events

The current territory of Romania has been inhabited since ancient times. Scientists estimate that the first signs of human life on Romania's territory go back approximately 40,000 years. "The cave with bones," discovered in 2002, is a system with 12 cave galleries, located in the Valley of Minis, near the city of Anina.

The oldest remnants of modern man from Europe have been discovered here. The fossils, coming from three individuals (named Bones 1, Bones 2 and Bones 3), were dated to 35,000 or even 40,500 years ago. In 2015, DNA analysis revealed that Bones 1 was an ancestor of Homo Neanderthalensis, with 5–11% of his genome deriving from Neanderthals.

During the post-Roman period, different waves of invasions of migrant populations crossed the Dacia territory (future Romania): the Huns in the IV century, the Gepids people in the V century, the Avars people in the VI century, the Slavic people and Bulgarians in the VII century, the Hungarians in the second half of the IX century, the Pechenegs, Cumans, Uzi and Alans in the X–XII centuries and the Tatars in the XIII century.

During the Middle Ages, there were no statistics on nationalities and only the toponymy and names of people provide information about the populations' origins. By the end of the XVII century, Hungary and Transylvania became parts of the Austrian Empire (the Habsburg Empire), while Wallachia and Moldova were Ottoman tributaries.

In 1718, an important part of Wallachia, Oltenia, was included in the Austrian Empire, being returned to Wallachia in 1739. In 1775, the Austrian Empire occupied the northwest of Moldavia, by then called Bucovina, while the eastern half of Moldova was seized by Russia in 1812 after which it was named Basarabia (before 1812, the name of Basarabia referred to the region represented by Turkey's ''Bugeac'').

Just like in many other European countries, in 1848 there was a revolution in Moldova, Wallachia and Transylvania. The revolutionaries' goals – complete independence for the first two and national emancipation for the third – remained unfulfilled, but they managed to lay the foundation for future evolution. The educational actions and ideas of the revolutionaries helped the people from these three princedoms recognize their national and cultural unity (e.g., language) and defend their common interests. These awakened national ideals lead 10 years later to the simultaneous election of the same prince in both Wallachia and Moldova, thus creating their defacto union as a temporary personal union in spite of the opposition of all European great powers and of the Ottoman government.

In 1866, the German Prince Carol of Hohenzollern-Sigmaringen was proclaimed ruling prince to provide German support for a full fledged union (legislative, judicial and administrative) and for obtaining independence in Romania. In 1877, Carol led the modernized Romanian army in the War of Independence, which was a resounding success. In 1881, he was crowned the King of Romania.

Source: wikimedia.org

Romanian involvement in the war from 1877–1878 and obtaining its independence as a state meant international equality with all other sovereign states. This held a profound moral significance as it raised the consciousness of a free Romanian people as well as encouraged the Great Union from 1918. More importantly, it contributed greatly to freeing the other Balkan states from Ottoman domination, making a decisive contribution to their evolution as modern states.

The new state situated at the confluence of the Ottoman, Austro-Hungarian and Russian Empires, with Slavic neighbors on three sides, looked to the west, mainly France and Germany, for its own cultural, educational and administrative patterns.

In 1916, Romania entered the First World War on the Entente side. Despite the military failures of Romania from 1916, which firstly led to the occupation of the southern part of the country by the German army and then – in the spring of 1918 – to the signing of a separate peace agreement with the Central Powers, by the end of the war, the Austro-Hungary, Russian and Ottoman Empires had disappeared. The representative bodies created in Transylvania, Basarabia and Bucovina chose to unite with Romania, resulting in The Great Romania.

During the inter-war period, Romania had one of the greatest economic rises in the world (around 5.5%/year). Owing to its great oil reserves and investment in the oil industry, Romania ranked in first place in Europe and sixth in the world in oil production (1936) and second in its production of natural gases (1937).

Further, Romania ranked high in gold production, second place in Europe after Sweden. During 1938–1939, Romania provided approximately 80% of its own industrial goods, producing a great quantity of oil, oil installations, buses and engines. Another great achievement of Romanian industry was the production of IAR 80 and IAR 81 airplanes (stirieconomice.ro).

The downturn of this prosperous society started in 1940 at the beginning of WWII, when Romania lost territory to both the East and the West. In June 1940, following the German–Soviet treaty, the Soviet Union attached Basarabia, the North of Bucovina and Herta.

Through the Vienna Dictate, Romania was forced, in August 1940, to give Hungary the northern and eastern parts of Transylvania in exchange for security guarantees from Germany and Italy. In addition, through the Treaty of Craiova, Bulgaria was given – following Hitler's insistence – two counties of south

Dobrogea: Durostor and Caliacra.

Romania entered WWII together with the Axis powers, in June 1941, with the aim to regain its territories lost to the Soviet Union, a fact initially achieved between July and August 1941.

Source: ww2days.com

On 23rd August 1944, King Mihai, supported by the opposition parties and representatives of the army, switched the Romanian army to the Allies' side, without having signed any prior agreement with them.

The Soviet army sought revenge on the Romanian military that had previously fought against it on the eastern front.

By the end of WWII, the northern part of Transylvania returned to Romania, whereas north of Bucovina, Basarabia, Herta and south of Dobrogea remained with the USSR and Bulgaria. Part of these territories, together with some of the USSR, constituted the RSS Moldova, a state that became independent in 1991 under the name of the Republic of Moldova. Following WWII, the Soviet Union strongly insisted on including representatives of the Communist Party from Romania in post-war governments.

Romania Administrative Map - 1966

Source: casa-regala.blogspot.ro

In 1947–1989, Romania was officially known first as the Romanian Popular Republic and the Socialist Republic of Romania later. In this period, the

Communist Party was the single political party, which imposed through its government its totalitarian rule on public life in Romania.

Geographically speaking, Romania had no capitalist neighboring state. Despite that, the communist regime was difficult to impose here. Indeed, paramilitary resistance continued in the mountains for about 10 years after the installation of the communist regime (Bohian, 2006).

Nicolae Ceauşescu was elected the new Secretary General of the Communist Party of Romania in 1965 and head of state in 1967. His denouncement of the Soviet invasion in Czechoslovakia in 1968 and brief relaxation of internal repression helped the new communist leader from Bucharest create a positive impression in the country as well as in the West. Rapid economic growth supported by great funding from the Occident did not materialize, however, leading to austerity and internal repression. The December 1989 Revolution lead to the fall of the communist regime in Romania.

A detailed analysis of the crimes committed by the communist regime was provided in April 2006 in the "Tismaneanu Report." These included the following 21 points:

1. Abandonment of national interests through servility towards the USSR after 1945;
2. Annihilation of the rule of law and of pluralism through setups and frauds, especially after the elections fraud in November 1946;
3. Destruction of political parties through the

arrest of leaders and militants;

4. Imposing a dictatorial and totalitarian regime completely dependent on Moscow and hostile towards Romania's own national, political and cultural values and interests; liquidation of trade unions; destruction of democracy as a political movement opposed to Bolshevism;

5. The complete "Sovietization" of Romania and enforcement of a despotic political system, led by a communist party group closely knitted around its supreme leader;

6. Social cleansing (physical liquidation/ abolishment through assassination, deportment and imprisonment) and forced labor, leading to between 500,000 and 2 million victims;

7. Persecution of ethnic, cultural, religious and sexual orientation minorities;

8. Organized extermination of political detainees;

9. Extermination of partisan groups (e.g., anticommunist armed resistance in the mountains);

10. Repression of worship and eradication of the United Romanian Church (Greco-Catholic);

11. Detention, killing, political imprisonment and deportation of peasants opposed to collectivization;

12. Extermination, ethnic suppression, expulsion and "selling" of Jews and Germans;

13. Repression against culture, extreme censorship, detention and humiliation of intellectuals not enrolled or protesting (1945–1989);

14. Repression of movements and students' actions

from 1956;

15. Repression of workers' movements;

16. Repression of opponents and dissidents in the 1970s and 1980s;

17. Destruction of historical and cultural patrimony through demolishment in the 1980s;

18. Building camps for orphans or handicapped children;

19. Lowering living standards (e.g., starving the population, ceasing central heating);

20. Conceptualization of moral and material misery to support communist power;

21. Massacring citizens upon Nicolae Ceausescu's order, especially during the revolution in December 1989. (wilsoncenter.org)

We are still fighting against the consequences of that period, during which the ruling power wanted to impose equalization by ruining spirit and personality – the essence of the Marxist trend.

For about 42 years they wanted to create a uniform society, without intellectual peaks. Indeed, the values and psychological attributes of the Romanian people are still, almost 30 years after the revolution, influenced by this mentality.

The revolution of 1989 was a bloody way in which Romania entered democracy. Many puzzles and mysteries remain unsolved, and the current government still has not managed to condemn those guilty for 1166 deaths and 3321 wounded people.

Religion And Its Significance For Romanian People

Romania has no state religion. Religious life in Romania is carried on according to the principle of the freedom of religious beliefs stated in Article 29 of the Constitution of Romania, together with the freedom of thought and opinion. Religious discrimination as well as the incitement of discrimination and hate are forbidden.

According to the Religiosity and Atheism Index calculated by the Gallup International Institute, Romania is one the top 10 most religious countries in the world and the only country of the European Union to be in the top 10. In 2015, there were 18,436 places of worship in Romania; 14,765 churches, 359 chapels,

1096 places for prayer, 47 cathedrals, two bishoprics, two mosques, 76 large mosques, 286 monasteries and 89 synagogues.

A diagram of Romania's religious cults according to the 2011 census is presented in the next diagram.

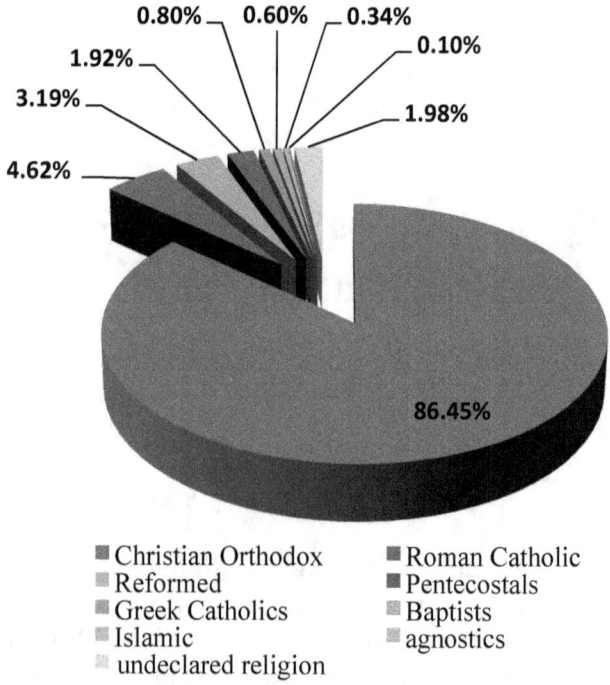

Romanians' religious beliefs are rather conservative: they believe more in creation and divine truth and less in scientific truth, feeling that the church has access to this truth and we must obey to it. Conservative beliefs are not associated with religious intolerance, however, and Romanians show rather flexible attitudes (Stan, 2010).

On the present territory of Romania, more precisely in

Transylvania, through the edict from Turda in 1568, the "Declaration of Religious Tolerance" was applied for the first time in Europe.

(enciclopediaromaniei.ro/wiki/Edictul_de_la_Turda).

Moreover, Romanians are one of the most superstitious populations among Europeans despite decades of atheism promoted by communism. Here are the 10 most frequently met superstitions in Romania (traditii-superstitii.ro/):

- If a black cat appears in your way, it means that something bad will happen to you;
- If your left palm itches, it means that you will give money away; if the right palm itches, you will receive money;
- If you break a mirror, it means seven years of bad luck;
- If it rains on your wedding day, then you will have a happy marriage and good fortune;
- If your left eye twitches, this means bad news or something bad is about to happen;
- If your nose itches, you are about to have fight with someone;
- If you want to drive away the bad luck or avoid something wrong happening, knock a wooden thing;
- If you whistle in the house, you attract bad luck;
- If someone appears in your way with a bucket of water, then you will have a very good day;
- For funerals, you have to bring a bunch of even number flowers, as there is a superstition that the deceased should find a pair in the other world. For

every other occasion in Romania, bring flowers in odd numbers;

- If you find a four-leaf clover, then you will be lucky and all your wishes may come true.

Cultural Differences Between The Historical Regions Of Romania

Although Romania is now a unified state, the fact that the four traditional Romanian provinces were separated from each other and influenced by different invasions constitutes the premise for different behaviors, attitudes and ideologies regionally.

In Romania, although there are many regional divisions, the most representative are Moldavia, Muntenia, Dobrogea, and Transylvania. The most important cities of these regions are Iasi, Bucuresti, Timisoara, Cluj and Constanta.

Whether a stereotype or not, the collective mind has it that Ardeal, being under Austro-Hungarian influence, borrowed some of the habits and ideologies of the

West; Moldavia, owing to its geographic location, has been influenced by the Russians; and Dobrogea, due to its Black Sea port and proximity to Turkey, but mostly its long belonging to the Ottoman Empire, has a regional culture influenced by the East.

As a consequence, the people from Ardeal are considered to be calm, but too slow, men of deep reach, but too self-conceited; the people from Muntenia are seen as clever, sly and capable of turning any situation in their favor.

The people from Moldavia are seen as poor and eager to rise in the social hierarchy, while those from Dobrogea are proud, easy going and party lovers.

Romanians are concerned about their appearance and the way in which they dress. Romanian women especially, no matter their social status, try to look neat according to their income. Romanians have a punitive cultural style, which can make them defensive, mostly caused by an inferiority complex (Ralea, 1997 and David, 2015).

Romanians have similar aspirations to Western countries citizens, but they are often unsure whether they are able to reach them. They have more pronounced mistrust than other nations in the state institutions. People are cautious about those standing for office, which might be a defense mechanism against possible deception.

Romanians' attitude towards the elderly is good and the values they project when raising their own children correspond to Western moral values.

A CURS analysis form 2005 (David, 2015) gave Romanians the following major attitudes: a craving for rapid enrichment, resignation, a thirst for justice and the power to survive and succeed through their own force.

Although Romanian creativity is high, the cultural level is not as encouraging and innovations are not adequately promoted. The educational and cultural environments have to be reshaped to capture and exploit the creativity potential. Many Romanians have become famous abroad: Mircea Eliade (US), Emil Cioran, Constantin Brâncuşi, Eugen Ionesco and George Enescu (France).

Regional Map of Romania

Map of Romanian provinces: Moldova, Muntenia, Transylvania and Dobrogea.

National Identity

Romanian people have a lot of traditions and habits, which accompany individuals throughout their lives. "Căluşul" is a Romanian custom on the feast of Rusalii (a Christian feast usually celebrated on the 50th day after Easter) and is connected to the cult of an ancient equine god nicknamed in the folk tradition of the Dacians-Căluş.

The Căluşarii tradition was born from pre-Christian pagan beliefs. In ancient times, the Căluşarii were actually priests of the solar cult. A great priest who became a bailiff after Christianity spread led them.

Nowadays, in the period of the feast of Rusalii,

Căluşarii wear a specific suit, with bells at their feet, and a bat in their hands. The ceremony includes magic formulae and practices, put into practice under a strict hierarchy: Mut (dump), Vătaf (bailiff), "ajutor de Vătaf" (bailiff aid), Stegar (color bearer) and regular Căluşarii. The sacred dancers reach a state of euphoric condition mystic cohesion by dancing to tunes played by fiddlers to the point of physical and mental exhaustion. From time to time, upon the bailiff impulses the dancers shouting some whoops. It was noticed that both the oath of silence and the whoops were having play an important role.

Latest researches in the field of energy have shown that for, as every word said is considered to lead the body to burn energy. Further, the whoops, according to their tonality and force, issue energy welcome2romania.wordpress.com).

The significance of this Căluşarii dance inherited and retained over years is to bring welfare to the whole community.

"Doina" is a lyrical creation (vocal or instrumental) specific to the Romanian people. The interpreter expresses his/her feelings of yearning/longing, grief, alienation, revolt, sadness, love, hatred against oppressors and regret. Nicolae Iorga, a well-known Romanian historian, said that the "Doina" is close to the term "torelli", as defined by the Byzantine lexicographer Hesychius, meaning a "shout or wail with the whistle of the Thracians" (Iorga, 1988).

Romanians voice their yearnings for those who have gone abroad, crave the glorious past and show nostalgia for time passed; however, the overwhelming feeling is of love and longing.

The great composer George Enescu said "our folk music, though bearing an oriental character, is completely answerable, through its sadness, to our native melancholy. It is actually the sadness even within joy.

This feeling is inspired by our valleys and our hills, by the special color of our sky, by the deep oppressive thoughts which at the same time give birth within us to a longing that cannot be well defined.

A foreigner who is my friend, hearing me one day playing a piece of my melodies, said: It seems that this composition has something within which cannot be defined. The yearning seems to me, the single original characteristic of the Romanian songs" (historia.ro).

The manufacturing of the Ceramics of Horezu is a unique traditional handicraft practiced by men and women from the North of Valcea County. According to the description of UNESCO, "men are those who extract the clay which is then cleaned, separated, washed, dithered, trampled and mixed, thus becoming the raw clay material from which the famous reddish pottery of Horezu. (...) Women are those who decorate the objects making use of different techniques and traditional tools, with the help of which they draw the traditional patterns.

The colors are vivid and vary from dark brown, red, green and blue until the famous ivory color of Horezu" (historia.ro). A prevailing symbol in the painting of the Ceramics of Horezu is the rooster, alongside other figures such as stars, snakes, trees, people, flowers, double snails, straight lines, fish, leaves, wavy lines, girdles, the sun, spikes, the tree of life and peacock tails.

Source: bucharestlounge.files.wordpress.com

An ancient custom still preserved today, especially in Transylvania, is that of the so-called three fates that appear on odd nights (3, 5, 7) from the first week of the life of a newborn baby and predict its fate. Tradition suggests that after the baby is born, even if it is in a hospital, the mother's relatives put calico, a pot of white flour, salt, bread and a coin in the baby's room to please the fates and predict good things such as a long and beautiful life.

Some Romanian figures well known among foreigners are sports figures: Nadia Comăneci, Gheorghe Hagi, Ilie Nastase and Simona Halep. In addition, the myth of Dracula is popular among foreigners. Indeed, as in the case of Romania's sports stars, the proud feeling of the recognition of national values is strongly felt by all

Romanians about Dracula (Vlad Ţepeş, Romanian ruler 1448, 1456–1462, 1476).

Romanians don't identify with the myth of the bloodthirsty character described by Bram Stoker. The myth of the superhero (as it is known by the Western world) is unpopular in Romania due to the realism, the conservation sense of Romanian people, which is why Bram Stoker story was not well received in Romania.

Given that Romanians have great respect for their history and ancestors, the invention of Dracula is perceived as an affront to the memory of a brave and honest ruler who loved his country and reduced corruption and crime during his reign remarkably.

He is still vivid in the collective memory, often invoked when Romanians face an injustice or are victims of an offence, as captured by the rhymes of national poet Mihai Eminescu.

Defining Romanian Spirit

Romanians have always had many traditions, fairytales, poems and sayings. Ethnologists, poets, writers and historians have tried for centuries to collect and save them.

Several traditions and customs are connected with different events in the year such as Christmas carols; the "Sorcova" a stick decorated with artificial flowers of different colors used for New Year wishes of luck and health; "Martisorul," a tradition that celebrates the arrival of spring; 1st April – fools' day; and "Dragobete" on 24th February – lovers' day.

The heroes of Romanian folklore do not correspond to Western myths with superheroes having fantastic but unrealistic powers (Pamfile, 2014).

"Făt-Frumos" is a positive character in Romanian mythology. In most stories, he fights dragons to free his sweetheart, the princess Ileana Cosanzeana. He possesses all the qualities of a hero: courage, justice, intelligence, steadfast love and always keeping his promise.

"Păcală" is a hero of Romanian wittiness. His name was derived from the verb "a păcăli" (to deceive). He is well known for his humor and quickness, hidden behind a mask of naivety and simplicity. He utters smarting truths just for fun.

"Bulă", a fictional character of Romanian humor, is not very serious and frequently gets into awkward situations, which he overcomes successfully. "He" appeared in Romanian culture during the communist regime.

"Prâslea" means the youngest son of a family; he is a hero who manages to save the day, due to his wittiness. He leaves for adventures with low chances of success and is laughed at by his older brothers.

"Haiducii"/ the brigands: some native legends talk about brave people who rob squires (people who become rich from exploiting peasants) and share the spoils among the poor, thus making things right.

There are many brigands within Romanian legends: some are fictitious such as Iovan Iorgovan (the native version of Hercules, the one who defeats a dragon), whereas others were real such as Iancu Jianu, Baba Novac, Pintea Viteazul, Andri Popa and Popa Şapca.

These legends with brigands lie inside every Romanian and are expressed through the thirst for justice and hope for a better future; these feelings have been gathered during the continuous fight for freedom of the

Romanian people throughout history.

Caught between the desire for the territories of our neighbors and repeated attempts to grow the Ottoman Empire, they have threatened Romanians' liberty, traditions, language and religion.

To better understand the spirit of Romanian people, below is a summary of proverbs and sayings that illustrate the experiences of Romanians during centuries.

Some of these are still used widely in everyday life:

Cu răbdarea treci marea – Patience wins the race.

Bine faci, bine găsești – Do well and receive well.

Dar din dar se face rai – Gift from gift, the heaven's made.

Răbdarea-i din rai – Patience is a heavenly virtue.

Fuga e rușinoasă dar e sănătosă – Running away may be shameful to, but healthy.

Graba strică treaba – Haste makes waste.

Nu lăsa pe mâine ce poți face azi – Don't put off for tomorrow what you can do today.

Țara arde și baba se piaptănă – Fiddle while Rome is burning.

Spune-mi cu cine te însoțești, că să îți spun cine ești – How you chose your friends tells who you are.

Lauda de sine nu miroase a bine – self -praise stinks.

Ziua bună se cunoaște de dimineață – A nice morning heralds a good day.

Degeaba ai trăit dacă pe nimeni nu ai iubit – Life is purposeless if you loved no one.

Bucuria mare îi cea scurtă – A great joy is the short

one.

Meseria e brățară de aur – A handful of trade is a handful of gold.

Omul vrednic se face lunte și punte și iese la mal – A hard-working man does what is takes to succeed.

Din trândăvie se nasc toate relele – Laziness is the root of all badness.

La omul sărac, nici boii nu trag – When the man is poor, even the bulls won't pull.

Ban la ban trage, și păduche la păduche – money sticks to money and bugs to bugs.

Omul cât trăiește învață – You are never too old to learn.

Cine se scoală de dimineață, departe ajunge – The early bird catches the best worm.

Cine sapă groapa altuia, cade singur în ea – When setting a trap for someone else you may fall into it.

Frate, frate, dar brânza-i pe bani – One hand will not wash the other for nothing.

Munca înnobilează omul – Work ennobles the man

Va ieși soarele și pe strada noastră – Good fortune will come our way too. (Junghietu 2013)

According to a survey carried out in 2005 (David 2015), Romanians believe they are best characterized by the following sayings: "să moară și capra vecinului" (The goat of the neighbor has to die also), "a face haz de necaz" (To laugh in face of danger) and "hoțul neprins, negustor cinstit" (The uncaught thief is an honest merchant).

Romanians' personality is a positive one, generally speaking. They are extroverted and have a sense of humor, thus managing to overcome hardship almost "unaffected".

The myth of the ballad "Miorița" defines the way in which Romanians' handle extreme situations.

The attitude of acceptance and resignation in the face of dead-end situations is almost unanimously recognized as the "mioritic" complex. The ballad "Miorita" is a Romanian folkloric poem on the territory of Romania, which has circulated into more than 1500 variants. It represents a synthesis of the life experience and mentality of Romanian people, standing for a philosophy of life and death and presenting the communion between man and nature. The attitude of resignation is always completed by the attempt to put a brave face on a dead-end situation.

The shepherd's attitude in the face of death is one of resignation and of peace, where death is seen as a symbolic wedding and rest in the middle of nature. The belief in fate is another feature of Romanian people.

To answer the critics who tried to reduce this ballad to one highlighting the lack of courage and obedience of Romanians, Rosa G. Waldeck, an American journalist of Jewish origin, said the following: "The most powerful impression that I keep about the Romanians is that they possess to the highest level a capacity to face the blows of fate in a relaxed manner. They know how to fall art-likely, with every muscle and every joint being soft and relaxed... the secret of the art of falling is of course, not to be afraid, and the Romanians are not afraid, as the westerners do. A long experience in surviving has taught them that every fall has its unsuspected opportunities and that one way or another they will be able to stand up again.

This is a people – mild, realist, settled by destiny at the border between occident and orient. Two thousand years of harsh foreign domination, of Barbarian invasions, greed conquerors, bad rulers, cholera and earthquakes and all these have led the Romanians the feeling of temporary and transient quality of things" (see Latham, 2002).

Psychological Profile Of Romanian People - Specific Values And Attitudes

The unfavorable geopolitical and historical context in which Romania has developed in the past 40 years has influenced the value system of Romanian people, which is represented by the following psychological attributes: tolerance, easiness, and attachment to family.

According to the Schwartz Value Survey (Voicu, 2006), the basic values of Romanian people are: security, universality, conformism, goodwill, tradition, self-direction, and achievement, power, further described as follows:

Human Values Priorities Romanian People

Security

Valorization of the safety and stability of the social contexts (risk avoidance);

Universalism	Understanding, appreciation, tolerance, equity, honesty;
Conformism	Confinement of the actions, tendencies, and impulses that could hurt others or to break rules and social expectations, obedience towards rules;
Goodwill	Concern for the welfare of dear ones, responsibility and loyalty towards them;
Tradition	Respect, membership and acceptance of the traditions, ideas derived from religion and traditional culture, acceptance of fate/destiny;
Self-direction	Freedom of action and thinking, freedom to create and explore;
Achievement	Looking for success, ambition, influence;
Power	Willing to chase social status and prestige, control or domination over people and resources, social recognition, authority;
Hedonism	Pleasure and personal

satisfaction;

| Stimulation | Incitement, novelty, spirit of adventure, presumption. |

If we compare these with other cultures (Western Europe and the US), we distinguish a value profile in which tradition, conformism and power have higher rates.

Therefore, the psychological profile indicates that conservatism and power are more striking than in other national cultures. For the other human values studied, note the lower rates for universalism (concern for general wellbeing), goodwill (concern for the welfare of acquaintances) hedonism (searching for pleasure), stimulation (looking for the new) and self-direction (autonomy, independence) than for the other European states studied (David, 2015).

A strong cultural indicator of Romanians is their lack of trust in other people, both known and unknown people, with the exception of family and relatives. This fact reduces the importance of friends compared with in Western cultures/countries, which show interest in the wellbeing of others (altruism), known (goodwill) or unknown (universalism) and own pleasure (hedonism). Romanians are devoted to their families and their work/job, which they perceive as being a means to social emancipation (David, 2015).

This might explain their affection and attachment to family and conservationism: Romanians show reticence towards divorce and abortion and persons with different sexual orientation, or different appearance, different race, etc.

According to the psycho-sociologist Alin Gavreliuc (Gavreliuc 2011), attachment towards family and the importance given to it are still encouraged in Romania, followed by the importance of work, religion and friends. Further, statistically speaking, there is no significant difference in inter-generational value orientation despite the social and political changes through which Romanians have passed during the past 30 years.

The Romanian cultural pattern is a collective one focused on family and work. Collectivism is based on cultural factors such as the need for security. In this regard, we can observe a generational difference: students' psych-cultural profile is more individual compared with the classic profile proposed by Hofstede and collaborators (2010) for Romania (David, 2015). Within such a collective culture, individual behavior is influenced by one's position in the group; the individual voices his/her wishes and goals in the shape approved by the group.

If individualism is associated with innovation, uniqueness and competition, collectivism is mainly associated with harmony and consensus. Bulgaria, Greece, Portugal and Romania possess a collective cultural profile among European Union countries.

On a scale from 0 to 100, Romania has very high uncertainty avoidance (90), which means it has a defensive culture. This is one of the highest levels in the world (China – 30; France – 86; Denmark - 23; Germany – 65; Japan – 92; Great Britain – 35; the Netherlands – 53; Russia – 95; United States – 46; David, 2010). This fact shapes the fact that Romanians see uncertainty as a threat rather than an opportunity.

Scientific research has examined the psychological attributes of Romanian people.

Analyzing the conclusions of these researches, we can notice, a consistency in the psychological attributes and cultural values as identified by different scientists along time – Dumitru Drăghicescu (1907), Ion F. Buricescu (1944), Mihai Râlea (1927), Constantin Rădulescu-Motru (1937) and Daniel David (2015). All this research shapes their psychological profile:

- Strong will, almost stubbornness, but impulsive and changing;

- A lucid intelligence that doesn't blindly follow religious beliefs, often derived from fear and obedience; this increased conformism brings obedience towards dogma. Religion is seen more as a means to do good for people than as a norm/religious ceremony. Romanians have a tolerant attitude towards those with different beliefs, as they see religion as a means to adapt to life and a moral support to face hardship.

- Inferiority complex: Romanians' low self-esteem is compensated by defense mechanisms such as neglecting the negative aspects or minimizing or emphasizing the positive ones. The tendency to avoid such situations could lower self-esteem, thus becoming rigid, difficult and vulnerable. Owing to restrictive beliefs, many times we are sentenced to fail.

- Indiscipline and disorderly work. Romanians leave things until the last moment and can work with huge effort to meet a deadline.

- Easily adaptable: an attribute that helped Romanians survive hardship of history, reducing the individualism and combativity in order to survive.

- A social, not an individual conscience.
- Conservative spirit and special consideration for traditions.
- Merry, funny and self-derisive. Capable of being tolerant even with own flaws.
- Welcoming and hospitable.
- Intellectual capability comparable with modern democratic cultures/societies;
- Superior creativity, but inadequately used;
- Highly competitive, mostly generated from the frustration of not getting the things considered to be fair or just for the sake of demonstration;
- Strong work motivation (involvement in ones work even against their social life). Work is perceived as a means to social affirmation and is strongly influenced by the fear of failure;
- Anxiety in women more than in other democratic countries;
- The need to show off (i.e., demonstrates welfare and luxury) as a consequence of low self-esteem;
- Tolerance towards ethnic minorities.

Romanian Inventions

1827   Petrache Poenaru – the fountain pen inventor;

1885   Victor Babeş - realized the first treatment of bacteriology in the world;

1886   Alexandru Ciurcu – built the first jet boat;

1895   D. Hurmuzescu – discovered the electroscope;

1900   Nicolae Teclu – invented the light bulb with power and gas adjustment;

1905   Augustin Maior – discovered multiple telephony. He succeeded to send five conversations without signal interference simultaneously on a single telephone line of 15 km;

1906   A.A. Beldiman – invented the hydraulic device with percussion chisel for deep bores;

1906   Traian Vuia – invented the plane with landing gear on wheels with tires; with "Vuia I" he succeeded the first take off without using any other auxiliary device, but only with the help of the onboard device (in fact the first plane in history);

1908   Acad. Nicolaie Vasilescu-Karpen – invented the "Karpen pile," which has been producing electricity for more than 100 years;

1910   Henri Coanda – the creator of the jet plane;

1910   Aurel Vlaicu – launched the first plane with a streamlined body;

1913   Ioan Cantacuzino – invented the anti-cholera vaccine and introduced the notion of immunity through contact;

1918   Gogu Constantinescu – discovered a new science, sonicity:

1921   Nicolae Paulescu – discovered insulin, the hormone produced by the pancreas that adjusts the glucides metabolism of lipids, protides and minerals from the body;

1929   Doctor Ştefan Odobleja – the creator of psycho-cybernetics and generalized cybernetics (the theory of systems management and their control through retro action);

1930   Anastase Dragomir – invented the ejectable seat;

1920   Emil Racovita –the founder of Biospeology;

1920   Gheorghe Botezatu – calculated possible trajectories for the "Apollo" training programs;

1952   Ana   Aslan – Romanian doctor in gerontology, has outlined the importance of procaine in healing the dystrophic disorders connected with the age, putting it into practice largely within the geriatric clinic, under the name of Gerovital or vitamin H3. The geriatric product was prepared in 1952 and got the patent for invention in over 30 countries;

1962   Ion Agarbiceanu – invented the first laser with gas (helium-neon) and with infrared radiation;

1974   George Emil Palade – Romanian-American cell biologist. Described as "the most influential cell biologist ever", in 1974 he was awarded the Nobel Prize in Physiology and Medicine along with Albert Claude and Christian de Duve. The prize was granted for his innovations in electron microscopy and cell fractionation which together laid the foundations of modern molecular cell biology, the most notable discovery being the ribosomes of the endoplasmic reticulum – which he first described in 1955.

1999   Eugen Pavel – inventor of hyper CD-ROM (storage capacity of 10,000 GB);

2000   Constantin Pascu – created a device to purify the air in living spaces;

2009   Company MB Telecom SRL – won the first prize within the International Saloon of inventions in Geneve with their invention Roboscan1 M, the most advanced system for radiography with gamma rays for lorries;

2010   Raluca-Ioana van Staden – invented a device endowed with a sensor capable of depicting four types of cancer (breast, ovarian, prostate, gastrointestinal) within the human body, from a molecule stadium, in less than 6 minutes. The device has a precision rate of 98%;

2017 Bogdan Mănoiu – invented the application iRewindprin with which one can record sport video clips from different angles and watch then directly on a smartphone.

The Romanians have a healthy national pride that does not prevent them from projecting as being part of one community or of the European Union.

Minorities In Romania

According to the 2011 census, the minority population represents about 11% of the country's 20.1 million inhabitants.

Romania – 2011 Population Census
Romanians vs. Minorities

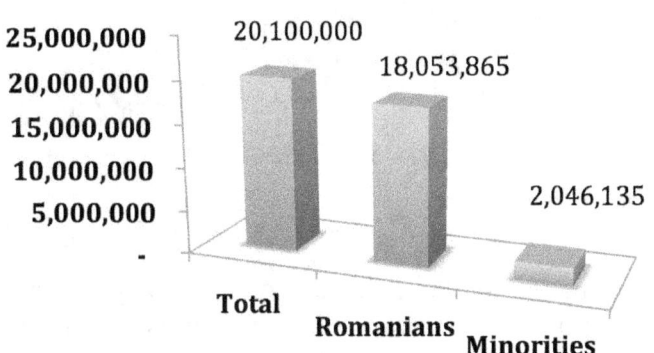

Romania – 2011 Population Census Minorities

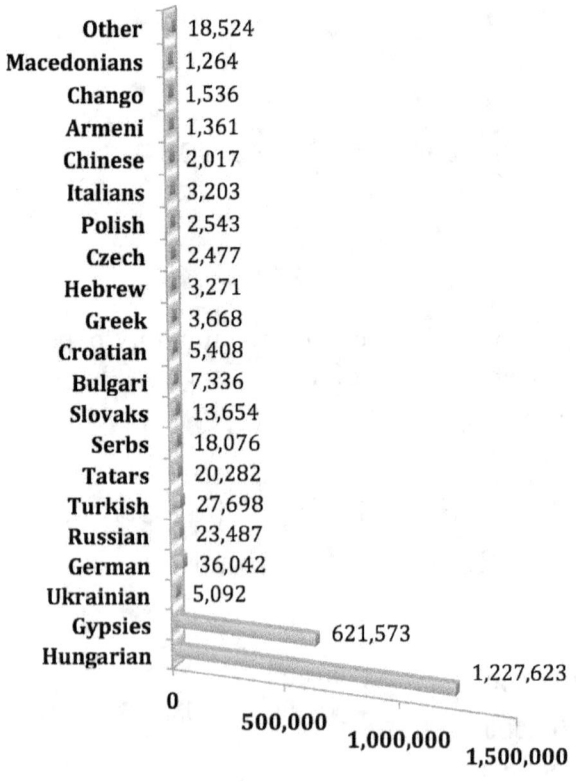

Other	18,524
Macedonians	1,264
Chango	1,536
Armeni	1,361
Chinese	2,017
Italians	3,203
Polish	2,543
Czech	2,477
Hebrew	3,271
Greek	3,668
Croatian	5,408
Bulgari	7,336
Slovaks	13,654
Serbs	18,076
Tatars	20,282
Turkish	27,698
Russian	23,487
German	36,042
Ukrainian	5,092
Gypsies	621,573
Hungarian	1,227,623

Source: Wikipedia.org

Romanian multiculturalism can be attributed to one of its provinces, Dobrogea, which forms the territory between the Danube and the Black Sea. This province has seen different dominations (Geto-Dacians, Greeks, Romans, Byzantines, Turks) and is currently inhabited by 14 different ethnic populations (gypsies, Turks, Aromanians, Greeks, Jews, Lipovans, Ukrainians) other than Romanians. This territory has been called "a miniature of Europe and Asia" (Constantin Brătescu) and is well known for its lack of ethnic conflicts throughout history.

The gypsies from Romania are, according to statistics, the largest number found in any other European country. They arrived in the modern-day Romanian countries at the beginning of the 10th century, brought by the Tatars that were coming through the Asian and Russian prairies and "they brought these people who served them as slaves" (G. Potra, 2001). They have found the Romanians to be tolerant and decided to stay.

The gypsies had few chances to be involved actively in the social, economic and political life of Romania due to illiteracy, thus becoming vulnerable to exploitation, poverty, unemployment, abuse and addiction to the economic social aid provided by the state.

The rate of literacy of gypsy women remains significantly lower than that of gypsy men, leading to the problem of gender disparity regarding access to education.

It is important to observe the RLM found in "Working Across Cultures" chapter of this book. This diagram shows Romania as a multi-active culture together with Greece, Serbia and others. On the contrary, the position of India for example (gypsies are part of Indo-European tribes) is opposite as a reactive culture.

Taking into account the characteristics of each group

together with the other aspects described here about gypsy people (illiteracy, habits not accepted by modern society), this may be the reason behind the lack of success of integrating the gypsy minorities by Romanian people.

Numerous other issues not accepted by today's society exist in gypsy culture such as marriage as minors, the ignorance or rejection of contraceptive methods and the lack of education even though access to education is provided by the state. All these aspects pose important problems in Romanian society given that the wellbeing of the family and children mostly depends on the mother's level of education.

The efforts undergone by Romania and the European Union regarding the integration of this ethnic group have remained unsuccessful because of corruption and the poor economic capacity of the country, and the ethnic group's reticence towards education and work as well as their self- sufficiency expressed in many forms (e.g., acceptance of and addiction to the social aid, refusal to find jobs, raise of their birth rate as a form of getting more financial aid supported by the state – addiction to the money given for minor children, and their refusal to go to work).

Iulius Rostas states that "being marginalized and subject to oppressions for many centuries, victims of forced assimilation and discrimination, the gypsies have developed their own strategies of survival, which make them different from any other ethnic group.

The Porrajamos experience – the equivalent of the Holocaust in the gypsy language – offered the gypsies the feeling of membership to the same community, no matter where they live" (Horvath, 2012).

Romanians' Work Style

The most common Romanian style of working is involvement in work competitively, sometimes even at the expense of social life.

Romanians are tolerant of delays and unexpected issues that may affect planned actions and value social status and recognition. Daniel David created a psychological profile of Romanian people characterized by the following aspects.

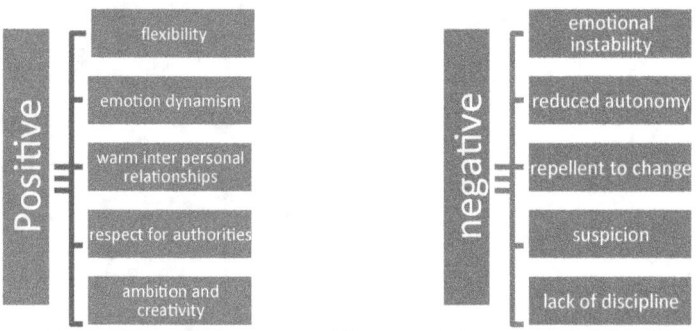

Regarding the Romanian work style, the research done by Jackson and Mavrogianuis – Gary/ Iliescu and Tănciulescu (David, 2006) establishes a high tolerance towards "put offs" or any other thing that may hinder the due course of an action, they are competitive and deeply involved in their work (sometimes even excessively until a drastically reduction of their social life).

These aspects are to be explained thoroughly by the fact that Romanians have an unstable economic environment for over 20 years. Further, for them, it is important to keep one's job and prove that you are the best. These attitudes are encouraged since childhood.

The communism destroyed the human action, responsibility and undertaking individuality, the promotion of the intellectual values and determined a collective cultural profile, and Romanians remain conformist and defensive which we still possess.

Things are constantly changing with new generations of parents raising their children according to modern society rules, but remains reminders of the past are very still widespread still.

Romanians' Communication Style

Romanians tend to adopt the defensive communication style specific to all collective and repressed cultures. They have a tendency not to say what they really think because of the fear of failure or marginalization.

But in exchange the values passed to their children are quite different. We note a change in perception in this regard. The phrase "No sword cuts off a bowed head" that represented the motto of the communist regime is now being challenged as more generations develop new habits.

Romanians are still learning the secrets of assertive communication and behavior, and they want to develop other communication skills to express their feelings, thoughts and beliefs directly, overtly and honestly.

They have the temptation/fear to suppress those ideas perceived as contradicting with those of their superiors, professionally speaking. Romanians face some difficulties expressing dissent without apologizing, expressing their intentions freely and being authentic and open without having to wait for validation or approval from those around them.

A stable and strong cultural indicator of Romanians is their lack of trust in people, both known and unknown, with the exception of their family/relatives. This is another trait from communist times when they were told not to trust anyone and not to talk badly about the communist regime, because people had been imprisoned for speaking their minds.

According to the classic Theory of Proxemics (Hall, 1966), different interpersonal distances exist: the intimate distance (0–46 cm), in which we accept without reserve for all close persons; the personal distance (46–122 cm), in which we accept friends, relatives and, all known people; and the social distance (122–210 cm), the for formal interactions and public distance (over 210 cm). Compared with the media in the other 42 countries/cultures, all these aforementioned distances are greater in Romania. For instance, the social distance accepted by Romanians would be within the personal distance for Americans. Maybe this is because Romanians feel that an unknown person has to prove certain things before he/she is accepted in the personal space, which is reserved for close people, friends. A Romanian has to be convinced his/her trust has to be conquered, while an American offers it immediately and all you need to do is to confirm it.

Half of Romanians can speak at least one foreign language; according to a Euro barometer survey 48% of Romanians can handle a conversation into a foreign language, other than their mother tongue. The top of their linguistics preferences is English followed by French and Italian. The verb that defines the Romanian people is "to have".

Within the business environment, the way of talking is impersonal. Many managers have concluded that their subordinates often adopt an impersonal language, to avoid taking responsibility, such as the phrases "we'll try", "let's see what we can do", and "it's possible", are quite frequently used in the business area instead of a firm way of talking.

This aspect may represent a reminiscence of the specific collective mindset of the communist state, where the payment was given to everybody, no matter of efficacy. However, Romanians also fear assuming the consequences in case of a possible failure.

Regarding the non-verbal communication, the foreigners who visit our country often remark on the strenuous, anxious mimicry of the Romanian faces, which are open and good willing to interaction.

Their gestures are many often ample, specific to Latin people, and expansive, as if to confirming their verbal language. Moreover have the tendency, if the report between the speakers is not official, to touch their addressee.

Romanians' Management Style

Daniel David defines leadership as a "process of social influence, in which one individual motivates others with a view to attain a common goal." According to Avolio and Bass/Iliescu in 2007 (David, 2015), Romanian managers focus on avoiding risk and monitoring mistakes. An intervention happens only if something doesn't go according to plan or if there are diversions or delays (management by exception).

Transactional leadership prevails, which refers to the financial motivation of subordinates through pecuniary reward, compared with transformational leadership, which is related to moral motivation through persuasion with ethical or spiritual arguments or motivations without financial rewards. So, Romanian managers may penalize employees if their work doesn't meet the required standards; they may also let employees control their income and provide challenges to encourage them to reach a greater level of productivity.

This style of management focuses on tasks with short deadlines and limits creativity and vision. As a consequence, Romanian managers are perceived as being cold, distant, controlling and not stimulating human interactions. Most are seen as selfish, focused on their own needs and showing different levels of grandeur. Managerial decisions are concluded because "this is what I say" and not by following consultation with specialists. They offer their subordinates what they consider to be necessary and not what the subordinates actually wish. They don't cooperate and constantly need to prove their superiority.

Regarding rewarding, Romanian managers have the tendency not to make differences, maybe even through rotation, without exclusion of those who are less efficient/ performing/ involved, in order to treat everyone equally regardless of performance and save their bilateral relations to keep/gain sympathy. Interestingly, Romanians have poorer bilateral relations despite avoiding disciplining those less involved compared with other countries where the rewards are small (available for more persons) and unpredictable (David -2015).

Particularities Of Romanian Culture

Romania has a polichronic culture. Our Latin belonging places us in this category. Combining this information with Richard Lewis' multi-active characteristics (Romania is situated close to the top of the multi-active side of the diagram), we can provide a clearer view of the specifics of Romanian people. Based on this diagram, we can observe the following about multi-active cultures:

- Communication and interaction patterns – indirect, showing emotion, lots of body language, promote personal relationships, relaxed about time, do several things at once, recognize authority and can be manipulative.

- Management/leadership styles – people-oriented, promoting personal relationships, important to be popular, diverge frequently from agendas, have intimate circle goals, intertwine business and social.

- Meeting patterns – diverge from agendas, often interrupting, talking most of the time, however responsibility is passed, and not easily assuming responsibility.

- Empathy – promote personal relationships.

- Trust – trustworthy, manipulative and diplomatic.

- Business ethics – diplomatic, display feelings, complete human transactions, do several things at once, plan grand outline, bad orders should be circumvented, find an excuse.

10 Important Factors Of Romanian Cultural Value

Based on the 10 cultural factors and value dimensions (Hall 1966, Livermore 2009, changingminds.org and culturaliq.com) we have identified the following 10 value dimensions for Romanian culture:

- Romanians still have a collectivist mentality from communist times; however, new generations are aiming towards individualism.
- High context – emphasis on indirect communication, tone and context.
- At least in the business settings, Romanians have

high power distance. They emphasize differences in status and superiors make the decisions.

- Romanians favor "doing and having" rather than "being". They emphasize being busy and meeting goals, which is important for showing status.

- Romanians have high uncertainty avoidance, which emphasizes looking for predictability.

- Romanians emphasize on specifics, unique standards based on relationships – particularism, although this is not openly recognized.

- Romanians are competitive. Their children are raised in this spirit; however, this trait makes it hard for them to work as one, and they only unite in tough situations. (Romanian community living aboard is one of the least united compared to other nationalities).

- Romanians are affective, share feelings and have expressive communication.

- They are short term-oriented, emphasizing immediate outcomes (i.e. success now).

- Romanian culture is polychronic – it emphasizes doing many things at the same time, with work and personal life combined, Romanians are comfortable with interruptions. Relationships are more important than completing an activity.

SWOT Analysis Of Romanian People

Strengths:

Labor force with reduced costs and an acceptable level of basic training;

Most people can speak English;

Openness towards professional reconversion.

Adaptable and hardworking;

Merry, good humored, satirist and self-irony;

Weaknesses:

Low level of research, development, innovation and a frail connection with the economy;

Poorly developed entrepreneurial culture, degraded and poorly developed infrastructure;

Indiscipline, disorderly work;

Fear of breakdown, fear

Strengths:	Weaknesses:
Hospitable and welcoming;	of assuming risks and avoidance of responsibility;
Intellectual potential comparable with modern societies from the West;	
Superior creativity;	The salary level is low compared with the national average, but the salary claims of the labor force are quite high in the context of the deficiency in the workforce;
High level of creativity;	
Strong motivation for work (strong involvement in work at the expense of social life);	
Work is perceived as a social assertion;	Decrease in the birth rate;
Tolerance;	
The new generation (under 20 years old) is largely open to change similarly to the people in Western cultures.	Eradication of vocational and apprentice schools with consequences on labor force expertise;
	Insufficient resources from the state budget for investment.

Opportunities:	Threats:
Ranks 10 regarding the population scale of the 47 European states;	Long periods of stagnation and economic decline;
A country with touristic potential and a strategic	Instability and inconsistency of the

Opportunities:	Threats:
position;	political stage;
The capital's modernization as well as that of other key cities;	Inefficient systems of tax collection;
Embracing the need for change;	Great quantum of the perceived taxes versus offered services;
Development of IT and	External migration of
communications fields and increase in the number of Internet users;	people with higher levels of education;
Development of the entrepreneurial spirit and of the IMM (small & medium enterprise) sector;	Climate change and environmental degradation;
	Rising number of vehicles and high demand for
Growing interest in formal and informal education;	transportation infrastructure, especially in urban areas;
Growth in the interest in ecological/eco-agriculture;	Continuing and increasing ageing of the population and rise in dependency;
Increase in citizen involvement within community life and the development of civil society;	
Increase in interest in sports and maintaining good health and a healthy diet.	Long-term unemployment rise, especially within the young population.

Leading/Managing A Romanian Team

On the RLM in "When teams collide" diagram, Romania is situated very close to the top of the multi-active part of the diagram. (see chapter: Understanding The Cultural Type – The Richard Lewis Model (RLM)). Therefore, the characteristics found by Lewis for these people are as follows:

- Talk most of the time
- Often interrupt
- Confront emotionally
- Have a good story
- Seek out key people
- Diverge frequently from the agenda
- Indirect, manipulative
- Diplomatic, creative
- Lots of body language
- Excitable

- Promote personal relationships
- Complete human transactions
- Display feelings
- Speech is for opinions
- Relaxed about time
- Have intimate - circle goals
- People-oriented
- Do several things at once
- Respect oratory, expressiveness, charisma
- Plan a grand outline
- Go for all-embracing solutions
- Intertwine business and social
- Bad orders should be circumvented
- Find an excuse

Most of these features fit perfectly the characteristics of Romanian people in general. There are, however, some cultural differences between historic regions of Romania and how people conduct themselves, although they are part of the same nation now.

The historic regions in Romania are Muntenia (Valahia), Moldova, Transylvania and Dobrogea. The differences here are mainly due to the influences of neighboring countries and that these regions have been occupied by different nationalities that left their mark on the locals (see the chapter Cultural Differences Between The Historical Regions Of Romania). Further, at a personal level, people may belong more or less to the multi-active category depending on their upbringing, education, age, personal experience and professional background.

Recommendations For Foreign Managers Working In Romania

Based on our experience of more than 20 years of providing destination services for hundreds of expats moving to Romania and having extensive expertise of working with locals, it is important to pay attention to the following aspects when working with Romanian people.

First, Romanian people are good workers: they work hard if they are properly motivated. Due to the stage of our social emancipation, our society is aimed towards "having" rather than "being". For this reason, income is an important part of the motivation of Romanian employees. Maslow's hierarchy of needs can be applied to societies according to developmental stage. See below the combination between Maslow's hierarchy of needs and basic income (kreytor.org).

Romania covers the two or three base levels of the pyramid. One would think that for basic staff (or those earning low incomes), material motivation would be the best way in which to motivate them.

This is partially true. But taking into consideration that Romanians lean towards valuing personal relationships, are people-oriented and mix business and social agendas, one has to take into consideration this very important aspect as well when thinking of a strategy to motivate Romanian staff.

The importance of having a pleasant work environment where they are valued may be surprising for some when trying to find a good way of retaining Romanian staff. Romanians respect authority and look up to the leader figure, especially if they are foreigners and come with top knowledge and status.

Any foreigner moving to work in Romania has to be aware of the fact that Romanian people are well educated; most speak foreign languages, especially English and French, and most of the people working in the business sector have university degrees.

During the communist era (and still ongoing today), children were pushed to be competitive (competition for entering university was high). Hence, receiving a university degree was seen as the pinnacle in communist society given that work was leveled and no private initiative was allowed.

Foreign languages were highly regarded. Nowadays, especially in cities, a foreigner knowing English can do without a translator almost anywhere in Romania.

One important aspect for a new foreign manager of a Romanian team is the fact that Romanians tend to mix business and social life. This means that closed circles are often formed around Romanian bosses and subordinates, or between Romanian employees. These relationships are not only based on business ties; often, they are relatives or friends working together.

Although things have greatly improved, there are still habits left from communist times when personal interest and family connections mix with business independent of competencies. One will find these intricate and unseen connections to an untrained eye very hard to predict and control in terms of their dynamics inside the company.

They can cause disfunctionalities in meeting established targets, when hiring or firing, especially when responsibility needs to be assumed.

Avoiding responsibility is widespread, this is one of the reasons why "red tape" is so hard to overcome. This can be noticed in the way some people express themselves. They talk in impersonal terms and undirected language, this being an indication that the person is not ready to assume responsibility for his/her mistakes.

Some of this behavior also comes from upbringing, because, as children, Romanians are pushed into ruthless competititions where failure is unacceptable. There is no concept of recovering from failure and moving on. Failure is perceived as final.
So, in order to hide failure, often times they tend to avoid assuming responsibility.

Romanian business environment has changed a lot during the past 27 years.

The Western oriented business culture established by the expat managers running the companies in the 1990's has graually changed as Romanian managers tookover.

Therefore one can find a lot of particular approaches to certain business aspects such as: management style, decision-making, delegation, promotion and also employment of new staff .

Since Romanians value human interaction, it is important pay attention to the personality of each member of your team.

Though Romanians are open to socialize outside work,

a foreigner may find themselves lonely during Christmas and Easter because these celebrations are traditionally spent within family.

To communicate better with them, the manager has to understand them. A lack of local cultural knowledge can limit the ability to develop a local business.

This applies to any culture!

How To Become Culturally Aware

According to University of Notre Dame (notredameonline.com), there are several key factors that influence cultural awareness:

Communication skills: These are the most important challenges for a manager when working across cultures and something that can be observed first in a new environment.

Verbal, non-verbal and para-verbal communication elements of local people are important to be observed and understood by the new manager. It is always helpful to speak the language!

Openness and observation: It is important to carefully observe the local market as a first step. Always stay observant and sensitive; try to find out the values and assumptions of the local culture and behavior of local people in different settings (business and family life). Listen more than you talk!

Flexibility: Be flexible; keep in mind the bigger picture. Read between the lines and adapt. When you are in doubt, just ask. Celebrate differences!

Self-awareness: Always be aware of your thoughts in some instances and of your own feelings. Question yourself about what makes you feel a certain way, and try to understand and accept your own feelings. Acknowledge them and adjust to every situation! Participate – it is the only way in which to understand a new culture!

Foreigners' Impressions About Romania

Most tourists visiting Romania are impressed by the landscapes, national parks (reservations) and Danube Delta. They almost instantly remark about their poor or insufficient promotion in the media. They also appreciate the prices, which are significantly lower than in other parts of Europe. Some are pleasantly surprised by the traditions and customs of Romanians, and others are quite intrigued.

The lack of information sources and poor documented media campaigns are the main causes of biased opinions about Romania. These suggest that Romania is an undeveloped country characterized by depravity and crime, with extremely poor, uneducated and racist people. Most foreigners who visit Romania appreciate that they were wrong in judging us only upon rumors.

Though relics of the communist regime can still be seen around the country there is undisputable evolution towards European values and lifestyle. Almost everywhere you go, many Romanian people (48%) speak foreign languages, especially English and French and are very open to meet, socialize and share cultural experiences with foreigners.

Romanians are among the most religious people in Europe, hence the great number of churches and religious celebrations. Nevertheless, Romanians are among the most tolerant people in Europe, ready to accept any religious orientation.

Generally speaking, Romanians are open, sociable and hospitable.

It is always better to see for yourself when you are looking to form an impression!

About Us

OANA HANGANU – entrepreneur and cross-cultural expert with 20+ years' experience in working with expats in Romania. EMBA – ASEBUSS and Washington Seattle University, Strategic intervention coach (Robbins – Madanes). Personal development consultant. Expert in analysis and behavioral assessment (Zivac Behavioral Research Center). Expert in subtle expressions and micro-expressions in work and social settings. Verbal and non-verbal behavior. Lie detection (Paul Eckman Group LLC). NLP practitioner. Trainer of trainers.

VALENTINA DICU – Psychologist specialized in applied psychology in national security. Psychological profiler, expert in analysis and behavioral assessment (Zivac Behavioral Research Center). Certified F.A.C.S. (Facial action coding system – Paul Eckman Group, LLC). Verbal and non-verbal behavior. Lie detection.

We met in 2015 and connected from the first moment (in the elevator going to the analysis and behavioral assessment course). Since then, we have worked together as a team in various projects and discovered that we have mutual interests, so we decided to write this book together.

We believe we have succeeded in reaching our first objective that was to write the present book and use our skills blended with each of our areas of work expertise to open new perspectives about integrating the Romanian culture and the Romanian business sector.

We hope we have been able to clarify some of the "unseen" traits of Romanian people to help anyone interested in working here, whether looking to integrate into a local team, leading a local or diverse team or simply moving to Romania.

We believe that being culturally aware is a must in today's world. Cultural awareness is a skill that needs to be developed by anyone looking to understand today's multicultural work environment and looking to integrate into a new culture.

We provide cultural awareness and integration

trainings that can fulfill the needs of a company or can help anyone looking to relocate to another country for work or education.

Our training and consulting services include:

- Cultural awareness and cultural integration training for expats moving to Romania and for Romanians moving abroad to work or study.
- Cultural assessments.
- Cultural IQ – training and certification.
- Integrating culturally diverse teams – businesses consulting.
- Communicating across cultures, training & consulting.
- Spouse support – one-to-one consulting.

Our training and consulting can be offered in English or Romanian languages.

To find out more about our services or for a tailor-made course specifically for your organization, email us at the following address:

oana.hanganu@deltarelocation.ro

Best regards,
Oana & Valentina

Bibliography

1. Bohian, V. (2006). Românii – între Păcală şi Miorița, Acces Print, București.

2. Ernest, H. Latham Jr., interviu consemnat de Ion Longin Popescu, publicat în Formula AS, septembrie 2002.

3. Gavreliuc, A. (2011). Psihologie intreculturala, repere teoretice şi diagnoze romanesti, Editura Polirom, Iaşi.

4. Hall E. (1976). Beyond Culture. Available on Kindle and other devices.

5. Horvath. I, Nastasa. L. (2012). Rom sau Tigan – Dilemele unui etnonim in spatiul romanesc. Editura Institutului pt. Studierea Problemelor

Minoritatilor Nationale, Cluj

6. Iorga, N., Buzatu, Ghe., Spinei, V. (1988). Istoria Românilor: partea întâi. Strămoşii înainte de romani, Editura Ştiinţifică şi Enciclopedică, Bucureşti.

7. Junghietu. E. (2013). Proverbe şi zicători. Editura Arc, Bucureşti

8. Lewis, R. (2012). When teams collide. Available on Kindle and other devices.

9. Livermore, D. (2009). Leading with cultural intelligence. Available on Kindle and other devices.

10. Pamfile, T. (2014). Mitologia poporului român, Editura Vestala, Bucureşti.

11. Potra,G (2001). Contribuţiuni la istoricul ţiganilor din România. Publisher, Curtea Veche.

12. Rădulescu –Motru, Constantin (1988) Psihologia Poporului Român, Editura Padeia, Bucureşti.

13. Stan, L., Turcescu, L. (2010). Religie şi politică în România postcomunistă, Bucureşti.

14. Voicu B., Voicu M. (2008). Institutul European. English edition.

Links

changingminds.org

culturalq.com

culturatorul.ro

culturalconflict.wordpress.com

cunoastelumea.ro

enciclopediaromaniei.ro

historia.ro

livescience.com

notredameonline.com

kreytor.org

romanobutiq.ro

researchgate.net

stirieconomice.ro

traditii-superstitii.ro/

unicef.ro

welcome2romania.wordpress.com

wilsoncenter.org

wikimedia.org